Haiku Ha

By Erica McKinnon

Enjoy Reading!

ISBN: 978 0 86071 905 2

Published on behalf of the Author by

MOORLEYS
Print, Design & Publishing
info@moorleys.co.uk · www.moorleys.co.uk

Soft blossom buds shoot
Creatures stir from deep sleep
A membrane erupts.

Slimy pewter mud
Streams of geese circle overhead
Outburst of sunrise.

Sweet chorus of birds,
Striking cat sharpens his claws
Tree bark in distress.

Dancing frogs leap
White lilies shimmer and glow
Weeds strangle and haunt.

Choir of tweeting birds
Screeching reverberation
Tranquil in flight.

Deathly still, haunted
Bare trees not even a shudder
Car engine ignites.

Beating of the sun
Warmth and stillness of the sea
Explosion of bees.

Bird feeders brimming
Incessant chatter 'til dusk
Prowling cat pounces.

Little chirping birds
Greed etched on their minds
Garden fence all white.

A striking rainbow
Pale bright subtle shades to adore
Coat of many colours.

Bucolic hedgerow
Beautiful yellow berries
Warning, do not eat.

Slug slithers along
Mutilated leaves hang limp
Gardener gives a sigh.

Blanket of snowdrops
Angelic white, still sleeping
Walkers' paradise.

Lifeless shrivelled plants
Desiccated in the pots
Squirrel turfs them out.

Tall swaying grass
Content timid hedgehog
Startled by mower.

Scattered showers
Carpet of bluebells simply lay
Woodland wonder.

Fragile pure snowdrops
March over sparse woodland
A pale blanket.

Yawning daffodils
Melodious blackbird marks territory
Mischievous weeds.

Old church high on hill
Warmth of sun, daffodils bloom
A cloud of midges.

Peeping golden sun
Blithely ramble through meadow
Radiant children.

Sheep pausing to rest
Shepherd strolls crook in hand
Dancing new-born lambs.

Golden ball of fur
Mad Monty runs chases jumps
A dog, man's best friend.

Who's that on my fence?
The sparrowhawk sits and stares
A magpie prances.

On a garage roof
Two lively squirrels line dance
Somersault away.

Memories From Australia

Incessant chatter
Soft tapping on the window
Scornful bird struts in.

Spooky spindly trees
Frothy sea cascading waves
Kangaroo roadkill

Fragile tangled web
Spiders dangly legs entwine
Peering, camera clicks.

Striking pointed claws
Cuddly koala munching leaves
A safe sanctuary.

Proud fragrant lilies
Rows of dancing bright orchids
Strolling in sunshine.

Red delicious grapes
Twisted upon a tendril
Childs fingers cling.

Thick cloud of midges
Thin veil covers the lake
Skiffs go sailing by.

A cloud of silver
Explosion of flying ants
Help they're in the house.

Brittle swirling leaves
Later, mounds of squelchy mush
Smiling children dance.

Rickety farm gate,
Clambering back onto bikes
Scones and tea for two.

Building sandcastles
Trousers rolled up for paddling
Remember suncream.

Small ghostly flowers
Magically glide down stream
Children feed the ducks.

Weeping willow sighs
Children tread on crunchy bark
Playground comes alive.

Warm golden sun
Jubilation, loveliness
Church bells, confetti thrown.

Nestling on a leaf
Caterpillar emerges
Madam Butterfly.

Tantalising grasses
Swaying frolicking whispering
Let's play hide and seek.

Pink dreaming blossom
Golden sleeping marigolds
Squirrel springs from bin.

Leaning bold snowdrops
A terrace of white wonder
Children tiptoeing.

Tree standing proud
Bountiful vivid berries
Chainsaw gang arrive.

Neglected garden
Abundant weeds, stretched grass
Time to meditate.

Injured plump pigeon
Cat hisses, crouched by wall
Fluttered to Sanctuary.

Angry pewter clouds
Aggressive rain, rivers boil
Soggy carpets again.

Pitter patter rain
Pools of reflective puddles
Tears falling, homes flood.

The golden wonder
Of rich autumn leaves
Naked are the trees.

A coat of white snow
Slipping sliding freezing cold
Ice thawed, lost forever.

Muttering blue seas
Taunting teasing listening
A man overboard

Yelping scrawny fox
Saunters along the road
Cats dash for cover.

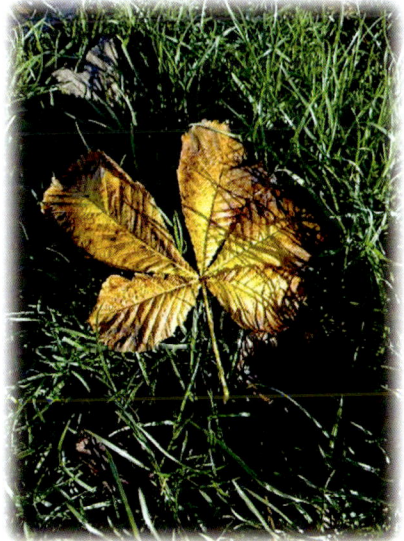

Trail of autumn leaves
Brittle crunchy noises echo
Hedgehog peeps and grins.

Proud robin red breast
Crisp white blanket of snow
Surprised snowman melts.

Fox footprints on snow
Screeching yelping marching by
Tiptoe to the door.

Pelting hammering rain
Cars submerged, panic rife
House on cliff subsides.

Whipping wind, leaves fall
Scattered all over the path
Leaf blower arrives.

Pebble grey moist sky
Arms entwined skates gliding
Children sniggering.

Taupe shaggy sheep
Silently ambles through snow
Sheep dog snores by fire.

Sleet tapping on glass
Temperature plummets, wrap up
Aroma of new cakes.

Sapphire sky, soft wind
Trees swaying in unison
Dog gambols, leaves fall.

Cascade of hailstones
Ebony sky, puddles glisten
Child stares, eyes wide.

Covid Pandemic

A quiet Christmas
Smiling faces, joyous words
Panto on demand.

Another grey day
Packed supermarkets
Lockdown is looming.

Meeting in the park
More restrictions on the way
Fed up, fed up.

It's never ending
More boring rules to follow
Covid go away.

Roll out of vaccines
Ease of lockdown, haircut soon
Have to wear a mask.

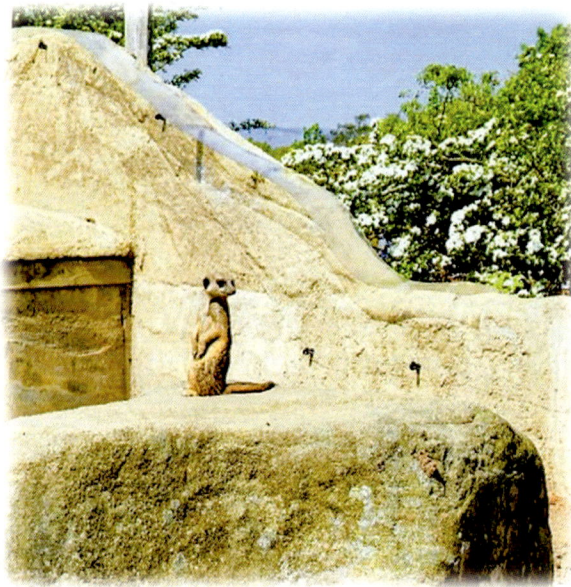

Be calm be patient
The future we take small steps
Today much brighter.

It's Halloween time
Trick or treat, rattle buckets
Scary faces smile.

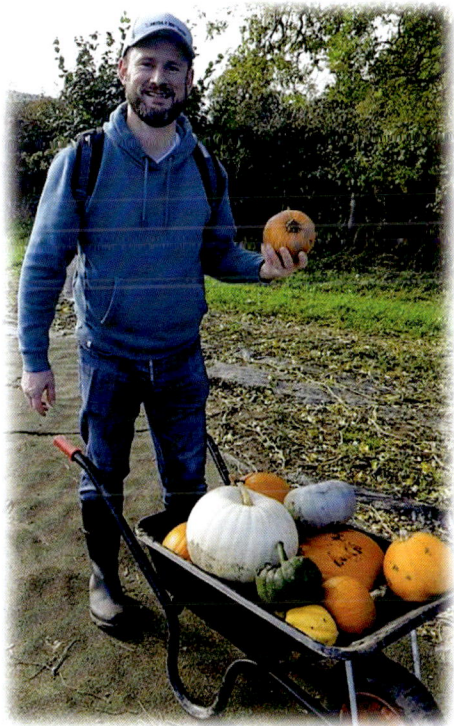

Field full of pumpkins
Gathered, carved then lit
Bucket full of treats.

Evening sky erupts
With vivid colour, loud bangs
Bonfire warm and bright.

Stillness of the night
Blanket of snow, sledge loaded
Santa chuckling.

Elegant fir trees
Draped in tinsel, radiant lights
Panto time again.

Ho ho ho ho ho
Swinging a brimming red sack
Child tugs at his beard.

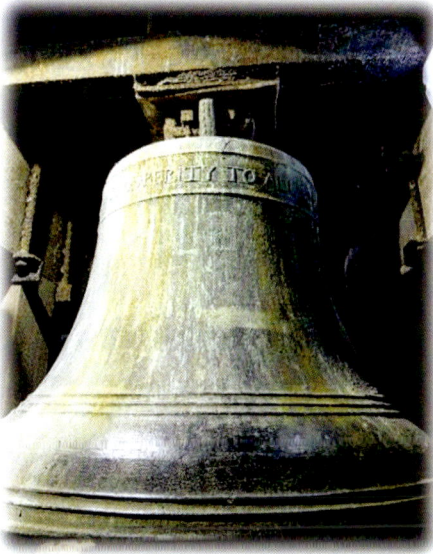

Chiming distant bells
Precious delicate angels
Darkness, silent night.

Singing with Santa
Sparkling bright coloured presents
Peeping red robin.

Footprints in the snow
Sledging, skating, carols sung
Eating Christmas pudding.

City of canals
Bell tower stands proud, we stroll
Warm sun turns to rain.

Bright Venetian sun
A gondolier rests, pigeons flock
Tourist crowds pass by.

A gorgeous sunset?
Perhaps the end of the world?
Magnificent hues.